MW01580488

DOWN THE GULLY

JAMES B. ZIMMERMAN

Black Rose Writing | Texas

©2021 by James B. Zimmerman

All rights reserved. No part of this book may be reproduced, stored in a retrieval system or transmitted in any form or by any means without the prior written permission of the publishers, except by a reviewer who may quote brief passages in a review to be printed in a newspaper, magazine or journal.

The author grants the final approval for this literary material.

First printing

This is a work of fiction. Names, characters, businesses, places, events, and incidents are either the products of the author's imagination or used in a fictitious manner. Any resemblance to actual persons, living or dead, or actual events is purely coincidental.

ISBN: 978-1-68433-787-3
PUBLISHED BY BLACK ROSE WRITING
www.blackrosewriting.com

Printed in the United States of America
Suggested Retail Price (SRP) $13.95

Down the Gully is printed in Calluna

*As a planet-friendly publisher, Black Rose Writing does its best to eliminate unnecessary waste to reduce paper usage and energy costs, while never compromising the reading experience. As a result, the final word count vs. page count may not meet common expectations.

Praise for the Meathead Series

"*Meathead* is a well-earned nickname because, if there's a dumb choice to make, Jimmy will make it. These stories are about being a kid; about dealing with peer pressure, about having a logic system with priorities completely alien to an adult mind."
-Dr. Jane Lindskold, *New York Times* bestselling author of the *Firekeeper Saga* and many other works

"The *Meathead* stories are thrilling, hilarious, and dreadful as he stumbles experiencing losses, celebrating victories, and searching for absolution."
-Jonathon Scott Fuqua, author of *The Reappearance of Sam Weber* and many other award-winning books and stories

"A sweet snapshot of a 1970s suburban American childhood."
-*IndieReader*

"*Meathead* stories are a fun read about the things kids try to avoid growing up and still turn out to be decent people. Thankfully, Jimmy went through it all and was cool enough to share it with us. Read it!"
-Kirk McEwen, 98 Rock in Baltimore

"Once in a blue moon a writer takes it upon himself to tell the story of what it's really like growing up crazy, goofy, loopy, secretive, schmaltzy, sweet, and sensitive. This book is a truthsayer."
-Gerald Hausman, author of *Little Miracles* and 70 other books for children and adults

"Zimmerman narrates short stories ranging from laughing out loud to a deeply saddened life of a boy named Jimmy. Beautiful crisp black and white illustrations capture perfectly the setting and emotions of the story."
-Andrea Tripke, author/ illustrator of *Miranda, Queen of Broken Toys*

Growing up Meathead was named as a Distinguished Favorite in the 2020 N Y C Big Book Awards.

For Mom and Dad.
Thank you for teaching us to dream big.

DOWN the GULLY

chapter one

"Come on, Meathead! Try to keep up," Bobby yelled, "It's not much farther."

My name is Jimmy, but all the kids called me Meathead.

Back home in the garage, my bicycle sat against the wall, unused. I would have to stick to my Big Wheel. I couldn't pedal without having my legs stretched like two chicken wings, though. The plastic three-wheeler under me was a couple of years old, but I felt safer on it than on my bike.

Rolling down the center of the road, with my feet extended, I passed by Eric and came up even with Bobby. The steep hill on Nolpark Drive was my only chance to catch up to them. But, as the ground leveled, even Eric passed me again.

Eric pulled ahead in front of me and caught up with Bobby. Bobby circled back once, glided through a corner lawn, and hopped off the curb.

"That thing's a piece of crap, Meat. Stop being a sissy and just ride your real bike," Matt said.

Ever since Dad pulled those embarrassing training wheels off the bike, I avoided riding it in front of my friends. I could get started easily enough, but my feet dangled a few inches above the ground when I'd come to a stop, even with the seat adjusted down. Most of the time I just tumbled to the pavement.

Bobby and Matt were excellent at riding bikes. They were way faster and could even do tricks on them. But they were both older than me, so I had an excuse. Eric was younger and smaller, but he could keep up with them on his newer Big Wheel.

Humiliated, I pedaled harder, but my two damaged plastic rear tires made clumping sounds as they spun along the black-top of Phirne Road. Both of the back tires had a worn spot where they flattened out, thudding every time they rotated, slowing me down and making for a bumpier ride.

"Go ahead, I'll catch up!" I yelled.

The rumble of my plastic tires rolling along the street echoed through the neighborhood.

"Let's head for the two black tunnels!" Bobby said.

I followed them onto the sidewalk, pedaling harder.

Running between our houses was a drainage ditch that ended in a small stream. Barely two feet wide in places, it was shallow enough to jump across without getting our feet muddy. In other spots, there were deep wide ponds. The stream started at the beginning of Phirne Road, fed by a storm drain. The round pipe poured a steady flow, mixed with run-off water, becoming a home for tadpoles, fish, frogs, and snakes. This was the gully.

The two black tunnels were at the far end of the gully. Fed by a second large stream, the swamp was wider and deeper at the tunnel openings. The mud was deeper, too.

We rolled down the hill and crossed the street, leaving our bicycles and Big Wheels discarded in the grass atop the tunnels.

The sounds of frogs and bugs chirping seemed to quiet as we made our way to the tunnel openings. Something ahead of us hopped into the water and splashed to the shade of the overhang.

"Muskrats!" Bobby yelled.

"Huge. They look like beavers," Eric said.

As usual, Bobby led the way. He had the rare ability to spot any animal ahead on our path and sneak up on it. If it could be caught, Bobby could catch it. He had a magic with animals, could talk to them—just like Johnny Weissmuller's *Tarzan,* or even *Doctor Dolittle.*

Bobby stepped into the muddy water and gave it a better look.

"They fled to the other side of this tunnel," Bobby said, "We'll try to catch em next time."

Exploring, Eric, Matt, and I scattered along the edges of the water. I spotted something bright red and yellow partly submerged in the deeper part of the swamp.

"Check it out!" I hollered.

"That thing must've belonged to one of the apartment kids," Matt guessed.

Matt and Eric tried to get to it from the opposite side of the stream, but that way was treacherous.

It looked partially intact, but the big front wheel and pedals were missing. The shape was unmistakable; a storm had washed the frame of a Big Wheel down the stream and stuck out there in the middle of its deepest, muddiest part.

"It's pretty slimy out there," Bobby warned, "We could sink up to our necks!"

Still, he made his way past me and splashed into the water a few feet from the edge, stopping when he was up to his knees, in six inches of water, but even deeper in mud.

"You try it, Meat," Bobby dared.

I hopped and skipped to avoid Bobby's failed path, then located stones and little islands of grass in the shallowest parts of the stream. I was over halfway to the plastic three-wheeler when I finally hit the slimiest mud. With a sucking sound, I went in up to my waist. In a panic, I pulled my foot out of my shoe. I had to reach down and explore with my hands to dislodge it. The icy water trickled into my belly button, so I gave up hope of staying

4

dry and waded and crawled my way to the Big Wheel. I tried to work it free where it stuck in the mud along with branches and logs.

"Snapper!" Matt yelled.

There was movement along the edges near Matt and Eric. A startled turtle with a shell the size of a man's head made its way through the muddy water away from Matt and Eric and toward me.

In a panic, I tugged at the Big Wheel, and with a huge sucking sound it plopped free of the mud. I crawled and splashed and ran through the stream, dragging my prize along with me.

The snapping turtle went into the muck. I once saw one chop a stick in half with its mouth. I sure didn't want it biting my toes.

The missing parts of the Big Wheel didn't concern me, because the rear wheels were intact, with full plastic tread on them as if they were brand new.

Standing on the side of the stream, covered in mud and filthy water, I cleaned off the axle and back wheels of the salvaged toy. Bobby helped me knock one wheel off and shake out the muddy water. With a little effort, we replaced the rear wheels and axle on my Big Wheel with the muddy new set.

We gathered our vehicles and headed up the hill toward home, leaving the scraps of my salvage job scattered along the grass and weeds.

Wet, cold, and stinking, I kept up with them this time and even took the lead on the last downhill run with my new rear tires.

chapter Two

"Remember, the ape isn't the good guy," I said.

We piled cushions to make support columns. We used a blanket swaying above as a makeshift canopy. My *Planet of the Apes* figure held a weapon to the back of a female captive. Bobby held *Action Jackson* up and threw a spear at the ape.

"Argh!" I yelled, as I tossed the ape and my sister's *Barbie* behind a pillow.

"He hides behind an enormous boulder," I said, "Cornelius is holding her hostage, so he yells, 'Give us money and your truck!'"

Then Bobby tossed his figure into the driver's seat, rolling a six-wheeled truck through the canopy.

"He chucks grenades and wounds Cornelius!" Bobby exclaimed.

As he made explosion noises, a furry creature startled us and darted under the canopy blanket, bringing the whole thing down on top of the figures.

Bandit circled around, then climbed onto my shoulder. He grunted and cooed, sounding worried.

"Hah! It's okay, Bandit... It's okay," I said, laughing.

The ferret bolted, disappearing under the blanket. His nose prodded my foot, then he sped around the room, making circles. He returned to my shoulder and snuggled beside my head.

"Just calm down," I said, petting him. Even though he was skittish around people, he wanted to curl up next to me. Without question, the oddest pet I ever had was this small brown ferret named Bandit.

He looked like a weasel, with a mask—resembling a raccoon's—and bounced all the time, grunting. He loved to chew things with his sharp teeth like a puppy. At first, he lived in an aquarium, but it wasn't long before we gave him a free range of the entire house. He found his way into the tiniest places, squeezing under doors, or making his way into tight spots behind the refrigerator.

Bobby was spending the night, which was always cool, but it terrified me that he would discover my dreaded secret. We made a huge fort in the living room since Mom let us stay up late. There were bowls of popcorn, half-eaten chips, and soda set aside behind us.

Most of my friends only had dogs or cats as pets. But not Bobby. Bobby had mice, frogs, turtles, and sometimes even a few gigantic snakes he'd caught barehanded. It seemed like he had a zoo in his basement. But even Bobby never had a pet ferret.

Setting the toys aside, we crashed on the floor. We made beds out of sofa cushions and blankets. Bandit slept on a pillow beside us.

"He really seems to like you," Bobby said, petting Bandit, "I wonder if he can kill snakes, like Rikki-Tikki-Tavi?"

It was Friday night, so we had the TV on channel twenty. Through the fuzzy picture and static, they announced *Creature Feature* would be on at eight. Introducing the movie was a goofy guy who played Captain Twenty, but dressed as a vampire.

"*The Wolfman* is coming on!" Bobby said.

Every couple of months they'd play our favorite movies, *The Wolfman*, *Dracula*, or *Frankenstein*. *Wolfman* was the best. The main character was a regular nice guy named Larry—but he got bit by a wolf. When there was a full moon, he turned into a wild and murderous werewolf. It was awesome!

We pushed aside our snacks and action figures and set up an area on the floor where we could draw. We loved drawing monsters, especially *The Wolfman*.

"He's got real mean eyebrows, like this," Bobby said, "and a nose like a dog..." He took the pencil and built up the face using familiar little shapes and shading. "Now you try."

I followed his directions and created my version. I wasn't particularly good at many things. I couldn't throw a ball as well as the other kids, I didn't run fast, and I could barely ride my bike. But I could draw. And Bobby could draw better than anyone I knew. He always taught me new tricks.

"Okay. That looks good," Bobby said.

Impressing Bobby with a drawing was a big deal.

I said, "Hey, you draw Evel Knievel, and I'll do Fred and Barney."

Once the movie started, we put the drawings down and followed the story.

"What's the scariest movie you ever saw?" Bobby asked.

"*Creature from the Black Lagoon*," I answered, "No. *Willard*. Definitely *Willard*. Rats really eat people, sometimes."

Bobby always talked about the movie *Willard,* where a bunch of rats pretty much ate a town alive. It gave me nightmares, even worse than when I watched *Creature from the Black Lagoon* when I was younger.

Rats and snakes really creeped me out.

Mom saw what we were watching and said, "Not *Wolfman* again!"

The movie was amazing, but being so tired, I dozed off around halfway through.

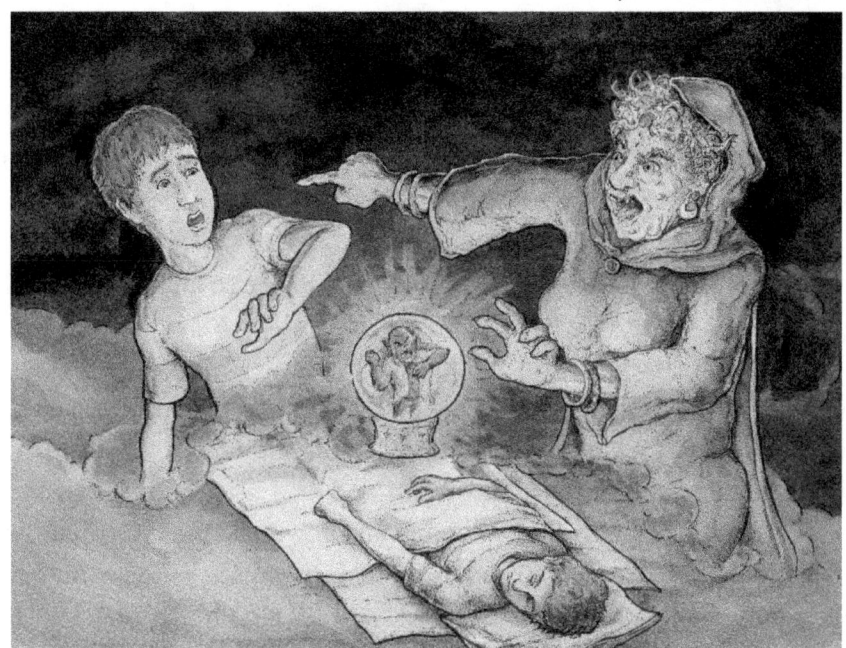

Dreaming, I talked to an old gypsy woman. Leaning over her crystal ball, she warned I was doomed to carry a curse, just like Lon Chaney Jr. did in the movie.

I woke up early, despite the late night. Along my left hip, I felt an all-too-familiar feeling. I rolled off the sheets and inspected the damage to Mom's good sofa cushions.

Bandit stirred and made himself a new bed near Bobby's feet. Thankfully, Bobby was still asleep. I snuck across the living room after gathering up the sheets, the blanket, and two cushions.

I opened the basement door, chucking the cushions down the stairs, then dragged the sheets and blanket to the washing machine.

Our dog Charlie must have heard me making noise, so he followed me down. I pet him on the forehead. He seemed jealous and clingy ever since we got Bandit. Charlie took the blanket from my hand and started tugging, He was thirteen years old, which is super old compared to humans, but he still acted like a puppy sometimes. Charlie was a great dog. He was a super smart mutt, a collie-mix. He was part of our family since before I was born.

"Knock it off, boy!" I whispered.

As if understanding I needed to keep a secret, he released the blanket and backed away from it.

I patted his head.

I looked at the damaged sheets and blanket. The gypsy woman in my dream was right: I was cursed. No matter how much older I got, just like my brother and sister, I was doomed to wet the bed.

I peeled off my damp and stinky pajamas and flung them into the pile of smelly, yellowed sheets and blankets. Mom had piled clean laundry beside the washer, so I put on new shorts and a t-shirt. I probably still stunk, though. I could never tell, after laying in pee so long that it would get cold.

Up on a shelf was a plastic bottle of baby powder. Mom used to dash it on me when I had an accident. I pried at the lid to get some out, then too much puffed and sprinkled all over me. Charlie snorted and even sneezed, then wandered upstairs to Mom's room.

Sneaking back to the living room, I laid down and pretended nothing happened. I would be humiliated me if Bobby knew I was still wetting the bed.

Charlie watched me settle down, and as if assuring himself I was safe first, then went back upstairs to Mom's room.

Bandit saw me and re-situated himself nearby. I patted his head, then pretended to sleep when I heard Bobby stirring.

"Hey, do you smell that?" he asked.

"What?" I said, horrified that he would know I peed.

"Baby powder! It's enough to choke on," he explained.

Sitting up, playing dumb, I said, "I don't smell anything."

Mom made us breakfast a little later, then told us to put the toys, sheets, and blankets away.

Up in my room, Bobby noticed a weird plastic covering that Mom kept over the mattress and under my bed sheets.

"Yeah, that's from when I was little, when I used to wet the bed," I explained.

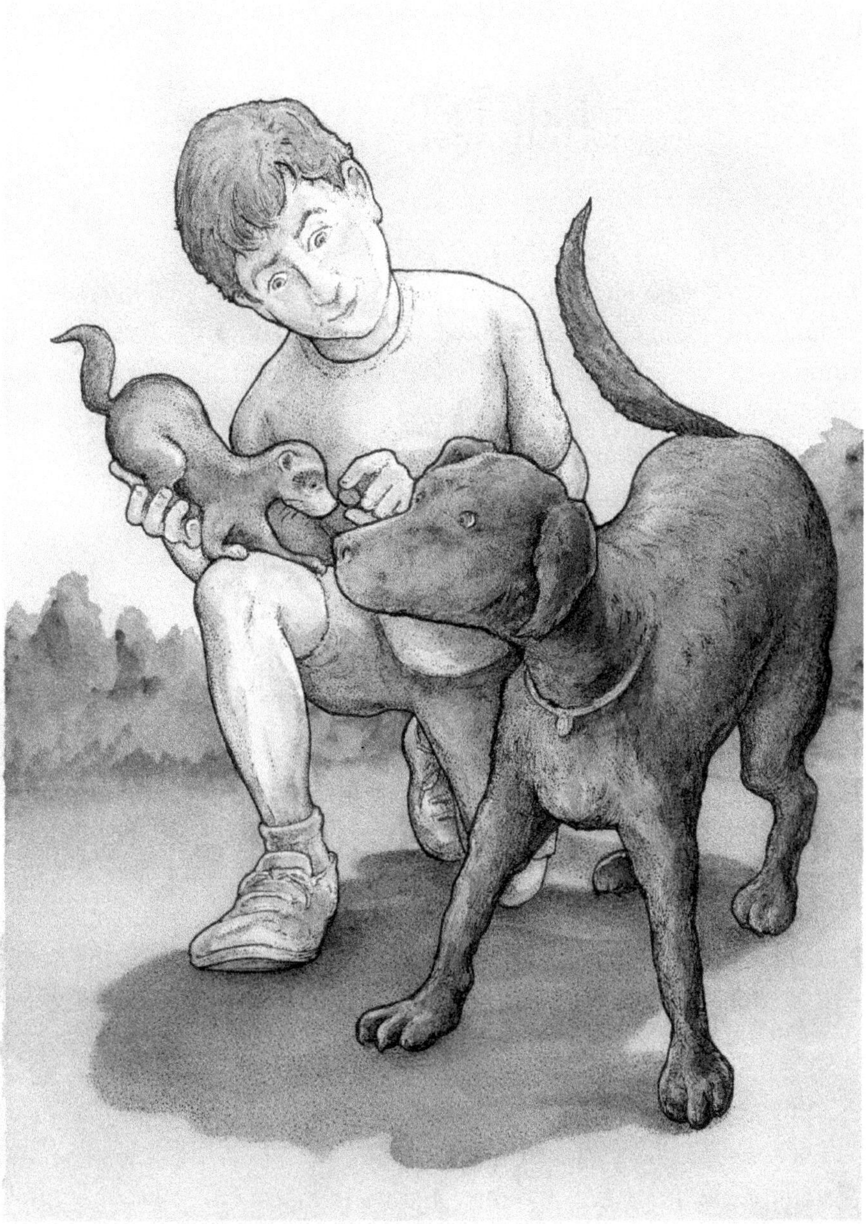

Chapter Three

Bandit was always energetic in the morning, so we watched him run laps around the garage. He tormented Charlie, stealing his dry food then running to hide it. No wonder it took so long for them to get along. But, after some time, Charlie seemed to enjoy playing with the crazy little ferret. Eventually, they even slept together on the couch.

"Where is he?" Bobby asked.

"There! No, there!" I pointed.

Fast as lightning, he ran through ten-foot pieces of pipe in a millisecond, like a hamster in a cage. Dad stored his electrical supplies in our garage, and Bandit treated the entire place as his personal Habitrail. He somehow turned completely around midway inside a piece of pipe and popped his head out the same hole he entered. He was so playful; it seemed he never ran out of energy until he'd crash to sleep.

"Come here, boy," I said. Bandit popped out the plastic pipe and leaped up onto my lap. I fed him a nugget of dog food and he took his time chewing it.

Hours later, Bobby and I took our toys out to the side of the house and played with the truck along the hill. It was pretty cool, rolling the six-wheeler into the weeds, but it always flipped. We pretended the weeds were a jungle. I pushed the truck too hard, and it rolled all the way down the hill and splashed into the shallow stream at the bottom.

We stayed down along the stream and played with our trapped our action figures. It was wet and dirty, but we loved it.

"My guy tries to climb out of the swamp but gets swallowed up by quicksand," Bobby said.

We used to think lava and quicksand were everywhere.

"Bobby! Lunch!" Bobby's mom yelled through the community. Disappointed to interrupt our play, he grabbed his things and reluctantly headed home for the day.

During dinner that night, Mom brought up my wetting the bed.

"You've practically ruined my couch. You're too old to be peeing the bed," she said. "You're going to have to stop doing that, Jimmy."

"Even Donny still does it sometimes!" I said.

My older brother Donny swatted a backhand at me, but I dodged it.

My sister Tina said, "I haven't in a long time! We do it because our family is mental!"

"I hate it. I never wake up, I just sleep right through it," I said.

Dad chimed in, "You should have to clean those sheets yourself! That'll teach you. I couldn't even sit on the couch today to watch TV."

As we spoke, we started raising our voices over the loud rumble of a huge seven-forty-seven jet flying low over the house. On cue, at the point when the plane was directly over us, the entire house shook with a roar and we all stopped talking. Jets like this flew over all day and all night long since we were so close to the airport. We were even in a direct line with the main runway.

"Jimmy, do the airplanes wake you up at night?" Mom asked.

"Not really, I'm just used to them, I guess," I said.

"You sleep like you're in a coma, because you're an idiot," my brother said.

Ignoring him, Mom said, "I just read in *Reader's Digest* that loud noises at night may affect the way kids sleep. They say it makes children more likely to sleep through peeing the bed. Let's try something different tonight. Sleep with the windows closed. And for the love of God, use the bathroom before you lie down."

Could this be true? Maybe it wasn't a family curse? Could those loud planes cause it? Even with the windows closed, the house would shake from them.

For the record, I didn't pee the bed that night, but I did the night after.

chapter four

It was the first day back to school, and my nametag kept falling off. Thankfully, I didn't wet the bed the night before. Starting school again was already scary, and worrying about kids knowing my secret only made it worse.

I was in second grade, and my new teacher was Mr. Fontaine.

"We'll start today with a fun project. I want everyone to take their pencils and crayons out and draw a picture," he said.

I interrupted him by getting out of my assigned seat and scraping my nametag off the floor by his feet. Embarrassed, I slunk back to my desk and struggled to attach it to my shirt with the safety pin.

"In this picture," he continued, "I want you to show me what you did for the summer break. What was your favorite thing about this summer?" Mr. Fontaine asked the class.

I loved to draw. This was a chance to show off in front of my new teacher and class!

I could have drawn pictures of playing on the beach, or playing with Bandit and Charlie, but it was more fun to draw monsters. Kids were coloring pictures of sunshine and grass and water all around me. Instead, I drew a werewolf, the way I'd been practicing with Bobby. We had the entire morning to finish, so I decided on an action scene. The werewolf was clawing at a woman. I even showed blood and scrapes on her face. Finally, I added in trees to the background, with the poor woman chained to a tree stump.

Mr. Fontaine gathered all the drawings up and laid them out across the desks at the front of the classroom.

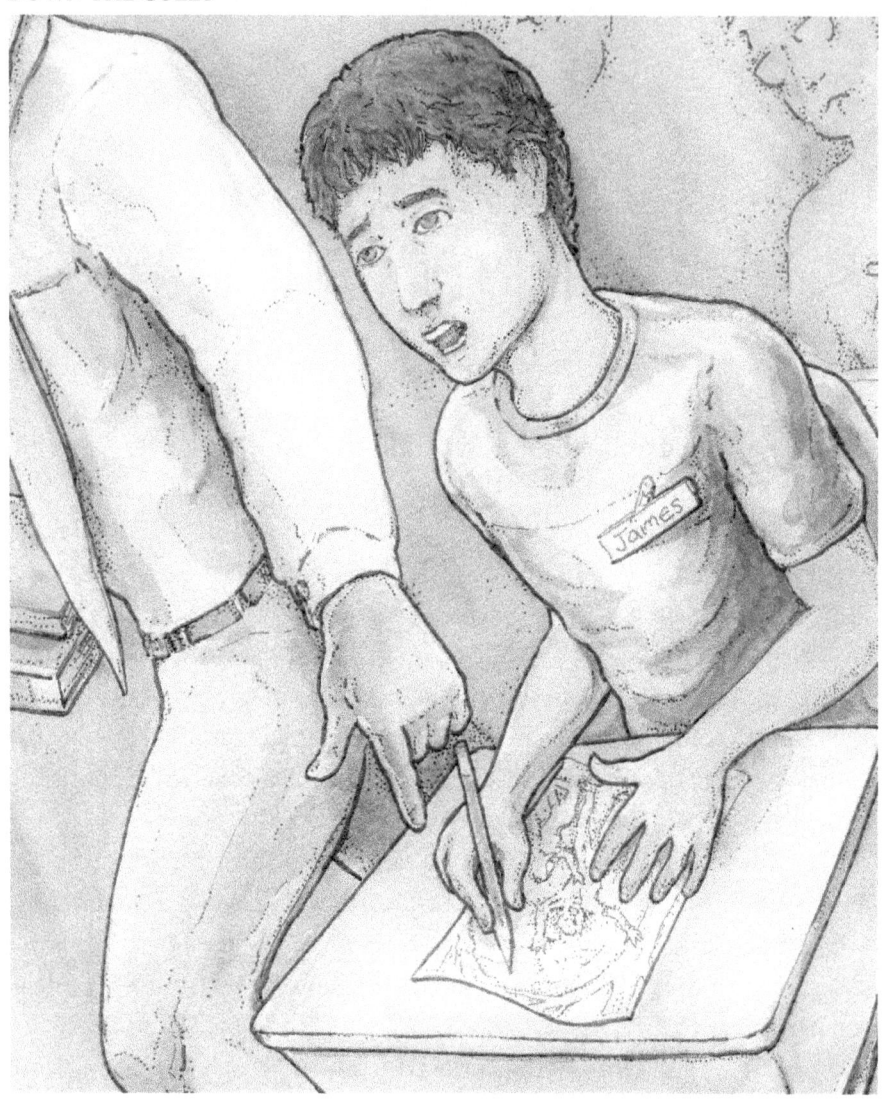

"Okay, we're going to have a little contest to pick our favorite drawing," he said, "Every student gets to vote!"

The kids clapped their hands in approval when he held up each drawing, but when he picked up mine, they broke out into a full applause.

Mr. Fontaine stared at the violent drawing and shook his head.

"James, did you become a werewolf this summer?" asked Mr. Fontaine.

"No. But I saw it on *Creature Feature* this summer," I said.

He seemed a bit disturbed, but he had to give me the award for the best drawing in class.

"You certainly can draw, James, but I think you need to work on following directions," he said.

That night, Mr. Fontaine called my mom and told her I had drawn a gory drawing and suggested that she might want to keep an eye on me.

chapter five

For a long time, Bandit slept with me and followed me everywhere, but he started developing some bad habits. Sadly, he would sneak away when we let the dog outside. He'd run for the fence and scamper under it, taking off for the woods. Sometimes he'd leave for hours, but he always came back. Recently, though, he was staying gone for days. Before I went to bed every night, I would go to the back door and call for him.

This time, I wondered if he would ever come home.

I was sitting at the dinner table with my mom, letting the dog finish off the leftovers from my plate.

"Don't let him eat too much," Mom said.

Charlie would have swallowed a chicken whole, if we let him. I pulled my plate back and he whined to complain.

After lapping up some water from his bowl, Charlie seemed agitated. He barked and whined a bit, trying to lead me downstairs.

"Jimmy, let Charlie out if you're finished eating," Mom told me.

Rubbing my hands on my pants, I headed down the stairway. Charlie ran alongside me, practically knocking me down the stairs. I spotted something moving at the back porch through the sliding glass door.

"Bandit! Wait!" I yelled.

It was no good. The ferret took a few pieces of dry dog food we left on the back porch, then bolted like a frightened deer when I approached. By the time I slid the door open, he was darting across the yard. Charlie followed me out the door and ran to the far end of the fence, sniffing around.

"He seems to want to live in the woods, Jimmy. Maybe it's for the best," Mom said from the door.

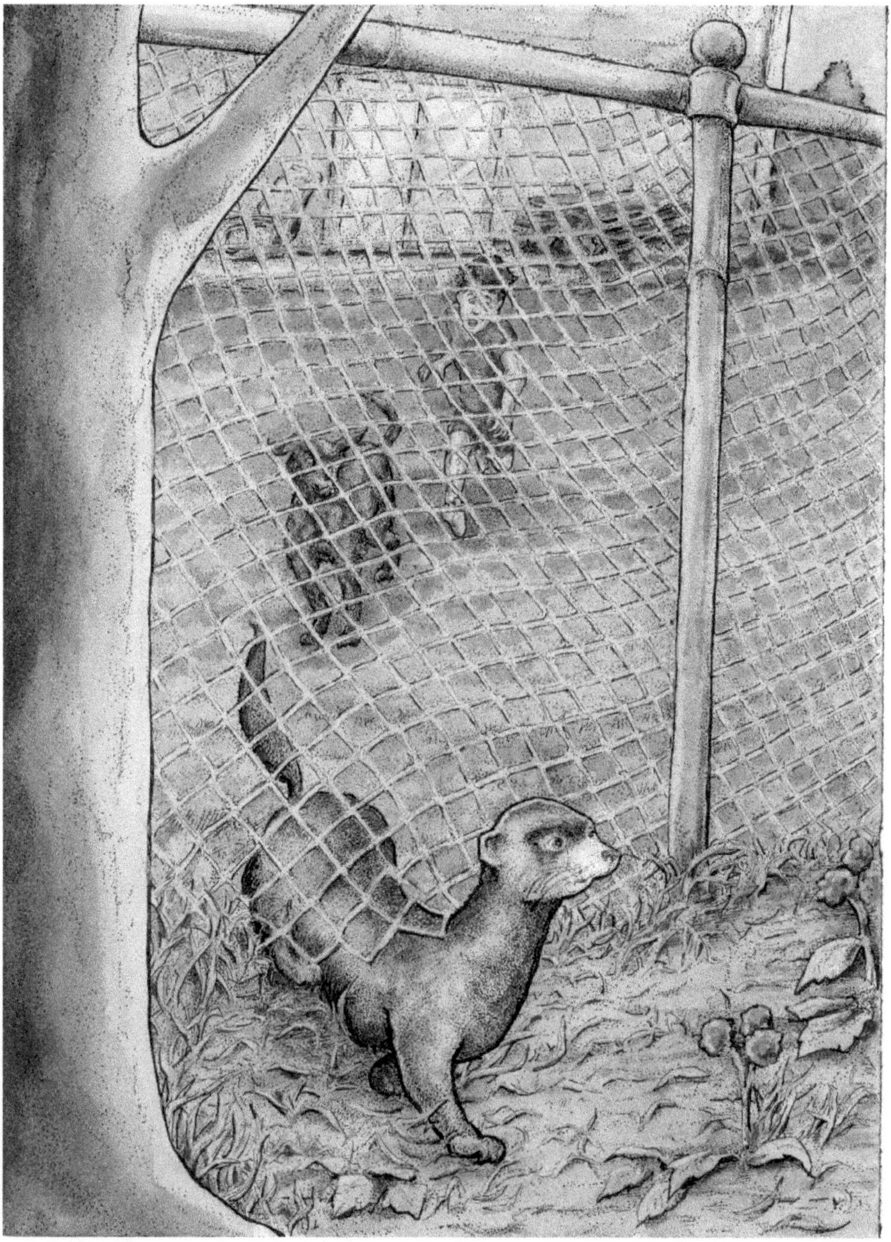

I kicked dirt and slumped my shoulders, answering, disappointed. "I'll keep leaving food and water for him. I don't want him to starve! At least we know it's not just Charlie eating it all."

I tried to lure him home for a few more days, but he stopped taking the food. Despite my many searches in the woods, he never turned up. I worried about him during the colder nights. Once winter came, I lost hope of ever seeing him again.

chapter six

I mounted the seat and let the bike roll down the driveway. Butterflies fluttered in my stomach as I grappled with keeping my balance while it picked up speed. I pedaled and controlled the bike, rolling in a long swoop around the court, then headed back toward the house.

This was the hard part. I lacked confidence as I pedaled to the front lawn. Coming to a quick stop, I tried to extend my feet and hit my crotch on the bar. The bike toppled over, and I went head first with it. I came down with a thud in the grass.

That hurt. Plus, more grass stains on my pants and a little rip on my jacket. Defeated, I sat in the cold grass looking at my bike.

Depending on my Big Wheel was getting old. I couldn't ride very far away with the other guys, and sometimes they'd leave me behind. I was ashamed. I was as bad at riding bikes as I was at baseball.

I walked the bike back over to the garage, ready to give up on it again. I leaned it against my sister's bike. Hers was a little taller at the seat than mine, but instead of a long bar running along the center of the frame, it swooped down toward the ground, like all girl's bikes did. I never understood why they did that. I guess they figured girls would wear dresses or something.

Her bike was purple with a white flowery basket on the front. I looked around to be sure none of my friends watched me. I took her bike to the driveway and hopped on it, letting the speed pick up to take me across the sidewalk and into the court. I kept my balance and rode it around in a few circles. As I let it slow down, I extended my left foot on the pedal and my right foot to the road. No problem. There was no frame bar keeping me from touching the ground.

I hated the flowery basket and the girly colors, though.

I took it back out, and this time I started pedaling from a flat start. Again, no problem.

A new confidence surged through me. I could do it! I made a few more quick turns and speeded up, pedaling harder. Ignoring my fears, I pedaled as fast as I could and turned around at the top of the hill. Soaring toward my house, I came to a successful stop at the end of our driveway.

"Jimmy! Get off my bike!" my sister roared. She must have spotted me from the window, and was on the front porch in an instant, "Wreck your own bike, leave mine alone!"

"Alright! Just shut up about it!" I answered.

Reluctantly, I put her bike back in the garage. I let it fall to the floor.

For the rest of the year, I barely even tried to ride the bikes, even though riding her bike was easier. I wanted to practice more, but I sure didn't want to be spotted by Bobby or Matt. I couldn't be riding around on a girl's bike in front of those guys. When the weather warmed up again. I knew I would have to stick to my Big Wheel.

chapter seven

It was early June, and school was over for the year. Matt and I walked for almost a half hour, planning to meet up with Bobby and his friend Michael. They rode their bikes to a pond down a long trail in the woods at the other side of our neighborhood. I rarely went this far from home. Mom was okay with us going to the two black tunnels, but she'd have been mad if she knew I was out of our neighborhood and playing near the community called Southgate. Still, we wanted to catch something new, and there was a great little creek we called the faraway pond that seemed to always be crawling with turtles and frogs.

Ahead was a pile of old chopped up logs and some two-by-fours scattered beside the trail, with weeds and mulch covering parts of them.

"We could use these boards for our underground fort," Matt suggested, "if we could get them back to our woods."

"It looks pretty rotten anyway," I said.

Further along the trail, we saw Bobby and Michael's bikes.

"They must already be at the pond," Matt said.

We tried not to make noise as we approached. The boys were already there, slowly stalking their way to the edge. Bobby took the lead, silently approaching his prey.

Matt stepped on a branch and it cracked, then in an instant, splashes, rustling sounds, and movements spattered across the water's surface.

"Huge!" Bobby yelled in amazement as he groped at the biggest frog I ever saw.

It launched three feet in the air, then disappeared into the deep area of the creek. A slither on the other side ended in bubbles along the water's

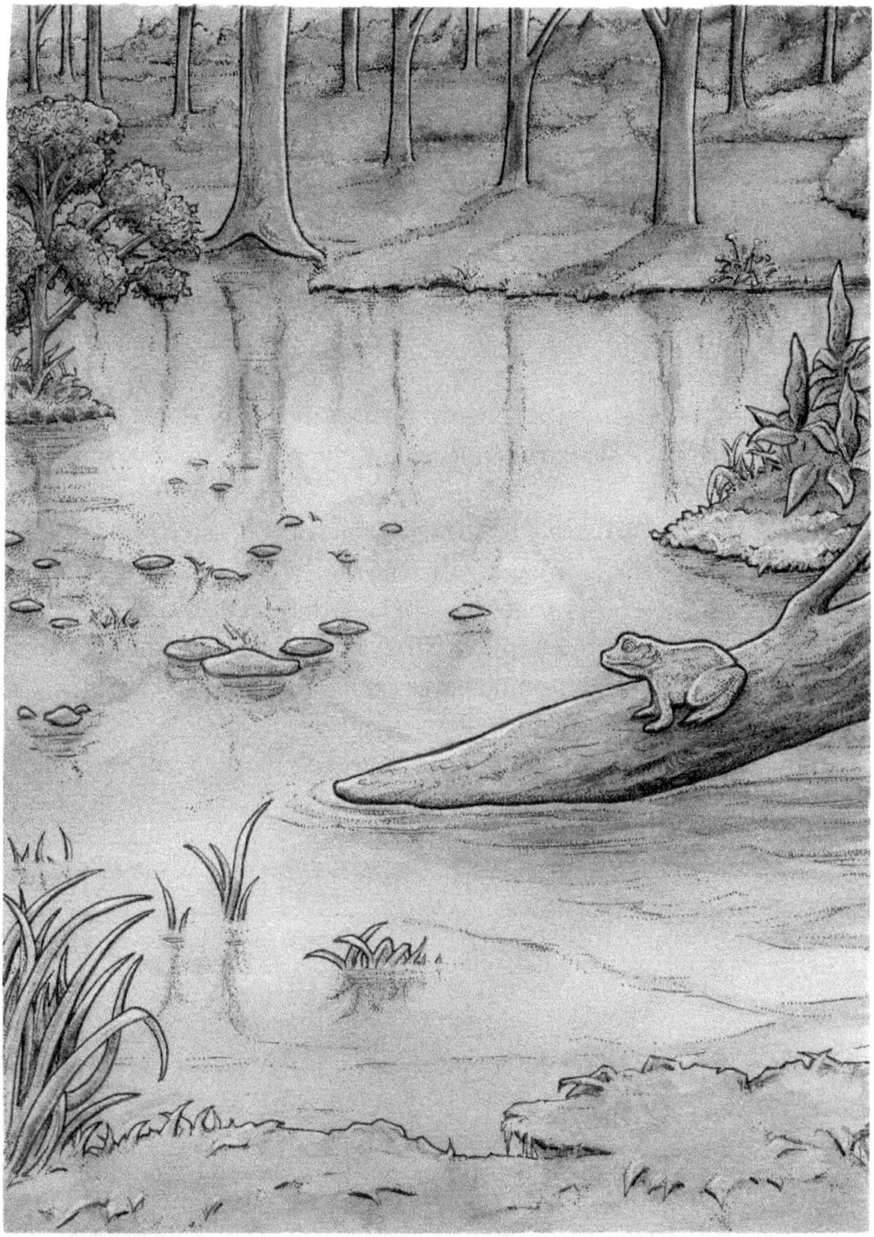

edge. Three small heads of creatures, either frogs, or snakes, or turtles, dropped below the surface at the same time.

Bobby cursed, then stepped into the shallows and swept his hand into the dark waters, coming up empty.

"You guys made too much noise," he accused.

"Wasn't me! It was Matt!" I answered.

"You just weren't quick enough, don't blame me," Matt said.

We waited for a few minutes and Bobby caught a smaller frog that resurfaced.

Michael scanned the woods along the edge of the pond, walked some twenty feet into them, and caught a closed-up box turtle that was hiding beside a downed tree.

I tried to catch a frog that popped up near me, but it slipped away.

We started back along the trail, even though Matt and I were empty-handed.

"That big frog was crazy," Bobby said, "I'm going to catch him one day."

"He was the size of my hand," Michael said, wide-eyed.

We reached the part of the woods where they stashed their bikes, but they hung out with us for a while. We'd try our luck again at the pond once things settled down and the animals got brave enough to come out.

"Hey, let's check under these logs," I said.

Bobby taught me a long time ago that critters like to live hidden under logs. We'd caught quite a few toads in spots like this.

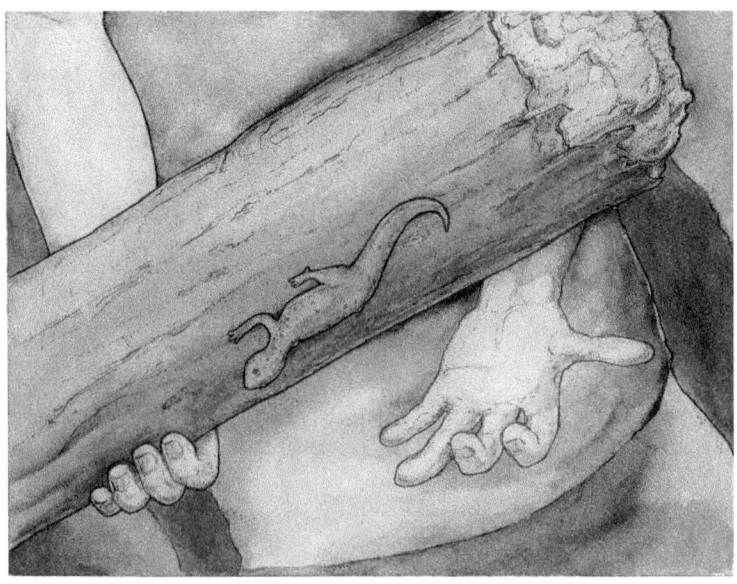

We stepped around the old two-by-fours and I lifted a heavy log and looked at the flattened damp ground under it. Nothing! I lifted a second, and again, nothing.

Then I looked at the underside of the log I was holding. A bright red and black lizard clung to the log, inches from my hand.

"Salamander!" I screeched. As I reached to catch it with my left, another hand darted in and swept it up, quick as a cobra strike.

"Mine!" Bobby claimed, "Good eye, Meathead!"

"No fair!" I complained, dropping the log. "That's my lizard! I was holding the log..."

Bobby ALWAYS caught the cool stuff. I spotted it, so the salamander should have been mine.

I stepped back once, twice... then it happened.

"You always get the... Argh!" I screamed.

My right foot pressed down onto a soggy two-by-four. The rotten board crumbled under my weight, and a long, rusty, corroded nail sunk through my shoe and deep into my heel. I wailed, falling to the ground, banging into other logs and boards.

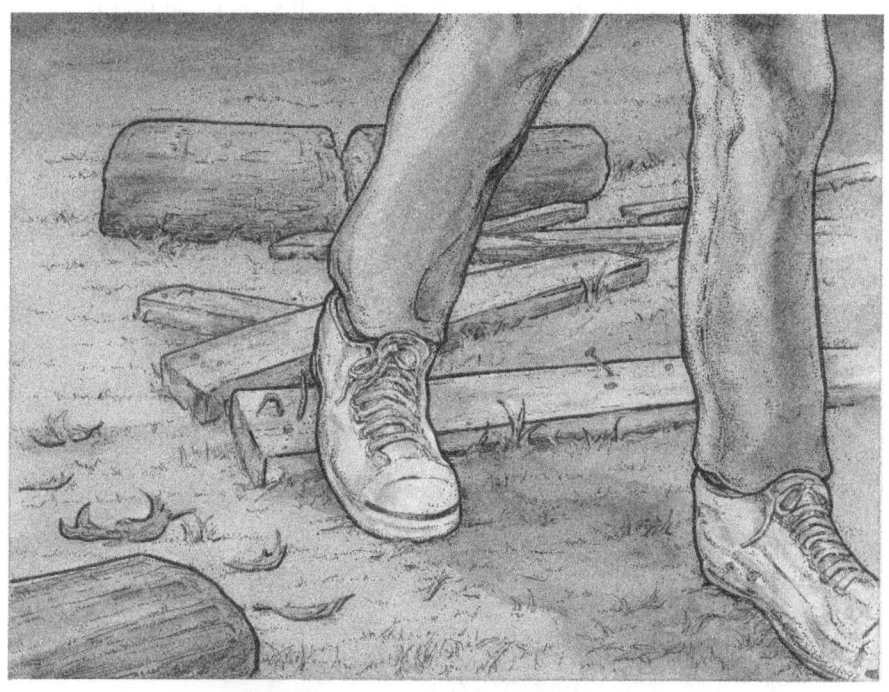

I howled in pain. The rotten board attached to me through my tennis shoe. When I lifted my leg, the board hung in the air, its weight excruciatingly suspended by the nail dug into a bone in my foot.

Bobby, still clinging to the prized salamander, rolled it up in his shirt front before he and Michael pulled at the rotten board. It finally popped loose, sending even sharper pains up my leg. They picked me off of the ground to stand, but I couldn't put any weight on the foot. Nothing in my life had ever hurt like this. It felt like a hot poker buried in my heel, while pain was vibrating through my entire leg like a massive toothache.

It was a long time before I got control of myself enough to stop crying. I could barely stand on one foot, so walking home was going to be out of the question.

Matt helped me pull my shoe off. Blood from my foot soaked the insides.

"If you can't walk," Michael said, "Maybe we should head back on the bikes and get your mom to pick you up."

I yelled, "No! Mom will kill me if she knows I'm this far from home."

Even in drastic pain, my mind reeled at the prospect of getting caught breaking the rules and getting into trouble.

My foot wasn't bleeding anymore, but it still hurt terribly. I kept my shoe and sock off.

Bobby came up with a plan. We used my bloody shoe as a cage. We put the salamander and the frog in it, then stuck the shoe inside my sock to keep them from escaping. Michael rode home with Matt holding the boxer turtle on the back of his bike. I rode with Bobby, carrying the animals in my shoe like a tiny sack while Bobby tried to maintain control of his bike.

I couldn't sit on the seat right, though. My poor foot throbbed and I couldn't keep it out of the way without sometimes banging it on the ground or Bobby hitting it with his leg while he pedaled.

We had to go pretty slow, but Bobby finally had me sit in front of him with my injured leg draped over the handlebars. On hills, Bobby stopped and just walked along with the bike, sort of using it as a wheelchair to push me along. I clutched the dirty sock full of animals, bearing the pain through the bumps and jolts.

When we finally got to my house, I told Mom the complete story about the rusty nail in the board, but I pretended it happened at the two black tunnels, instead of at the faraway pond.

"Oh my God, that's going to get infected for sure!" she said, examining my heel.

She took me to the emergency room.

This was the first time I could remember being in a hospital. A loud ambulance pulled up and people rushed out to help some guy with bloody bandages on his head. Other sick people sat in scattered seats, hoping to get help in the waiting room. Nurses and doctors hurried around, checking charts and seeing patients. It was amazing to see that so many sick and injured people waited for medical care. I wondered if it was this busy every day.

In pain, I sat there for hours, watching others get wheeled in to see the doctor ahead of us. Finally, a man in a blue pull-over shirt looked at my foot. First, he gave me a needle to numb it, then he jammed a Q-tip covered with orange medicine into the hole and swished it around. I tried not to cry.

"Rusty nail, eh? Looks like some of that dirt is still in there," he said.

He prodded at it again trying to clean it.

Afterwards, he used another needle to give me a tetanus shot in my shoulder, and it hurt, but not as bad as the nail hole did earlier.

Mom took me home, and I had to keep the foot raised with an ice pack on it. The worst pain came back about an hour later, and it was a few days before it stopped throbbing. But it never got infected, so Mom said I was lucky.

It sure hurt a lot to be lucky.

I was grateful to Bobby for all his help to get me home from the faraway pond. But that salamander still should have been mine.

Chapter Eight

"Let's catch some frogs!" I shouted.

It was getting hotter outside, so Bobby and I were collecting lots of frogs and tadpoles to keep in our aquariums.

"I'll get my bucket and meet you down the gully," Bobby said.

We met at the storm drain, where water was streaming out at a rapid pace. I shuddered when I looked into the darkness of that creepy tunnel.

After such a big storm, it transformed the gully. Now wide flowing streams with deep ponds coursed through the entire area. We were determined to catch more frogs or toads or—if we were lucky—a turtle or a lizard.

Bobby led the way. He signaled with his hand to stop moving. He raised his arm and pointed. The recent storm raised the level of the stream about six inches.

"Snake! A big one!" he whispered.

Up along the side of the stream, on a wet and grassy mound, a two-foot garter snake was curled up, sunning itself. Bobby approached slowly, then dashed his hand out, quick as a fox, grabbing the snake behind the neck. It writhed and coiled around his arm.

"Careful! You sure it ain't a water moccasin?" I jumped across the stream and said, "Just don't let it bite you! Could it be a copperhead?"

Bobby smirked, "Nah, it's just a gardener snake. He's pretty big, though." Still, he carried it with his hand clamped tightly around the head, to avoid being bitten.

It was actually a garter snake, but neither of us even knew what a garter was.

We went up the hill and to my yard, trying to find something to store the snake in to allow us to keep hunting. I pulled out a rusty bucket and a couple of paper bags from the shed.

"He'll just get out of the bucket," Bobby said. Instead, he dropped the snake into a paper bag, then quickly curled up the ends, double folding them. "I sure wish we could put him in your aquarium."

"No way. Mom always says, 'No snakes allowed in the house,' we'll just have to keep him on the back porch," I said.

"You want to hold him?" Bobby asked.

"No!" I said.

Bobby taught me a lot about animals, and I was good with them, but snakes terrified me, almost as much as rats. My brother Donny always warned me about the poisonous kind. Watching people get bit by cobras and rattlesnakes in the cartoons *Johnny Quest* and *Rikki-Tikki-Tavi* probably didn't help.

I wanted nothing to do with snakes or rats.

Bobby left the curled-up bag with the snake in it, sitting on the back-porch picnic table. We both were eager to see what crawled around the other end of the gully.

Walking with muddy shoes along the side of the stream, my socks were swamp-covered. I caught a frog before he could escape and added it to the bucket.

The storm washed away some debris under a tall oak tree a few feet from the water's edge. Water streamed through its exposed roots, forming a hollow spot under the trunk.

"Might be another snake in there," Bobby said. Using a stick, he prodded into the hollow. Leaves and dirt spilled out. Moving it back and forth, some strange reddish-brown nuggets fell to the soil beneath the tree trunk.

"It's dog food... It's Charlie's dog food!" I whispered.

Bursting out of the hollow, a wild creature bared its fangs. Larger than when he left and covered with a strange mingling of white in his coat,

Bandit confronted us with his back hunched up. Bobby fell into me, howling. Startled, Bandit made deep, threatening grunts like a tiny werewolf.

"He's alive!" I yelled, "Bandit!" I reached my hand out, but he snapped at me, looked confused, and then retreated. He danced and skipped backwards, bolting up a hill, and lost himself among the trees.

"He made a nest in that tree trunk. I can't believe he's been living here for so long," I said.

"He's gone wild," Bobby said.

We tried to follow him, but he was nowhere in sight. Giving up, we headed to Bobby's house to set up an aquarium for his new snake.

Bobby was right. Bandit was acting crazy, running around the gully like some sort of werewolf on a full moon. Maybe we could catch him, train him to be calm and civilized again.

Meanwhile, in my back yard, my mom was hanging sheets up to dry. I had wet the bed again, and she needed space in the dryer for other laundry. On her way back into the house, she noticed a paper lunch bag sitting on her picnic table.

"What in the world do these boys have in here?" she thought.

Halfway home, we heard the scream.

"Eeeeeeeeeeeyaaaaaaaaahhhh!" Far away, a woman shrieked. I did not know who it could be.

Bobby's eyes popped wide.

"My snake! She found my snake!" he hollered.

Curious to see what kind of lunch was in the paper bag, she picked it up to her face, unrolled the top, then... Bam! The coiled-up garter snake sprang out within inches of her nose. Mom fell backwards onto the bench as the snake slithered off the tabletop, through the grass and to the woods.

The snake was long gone before Bobby and I came around the corner to see the discarded bag. Mom emerged from the back door with her arms folded.

"Whose bag is this?" she asked, seething with anger, picking up the empty bag. Behind him, I pointed at Bobby.

"Bandit…" Bobby answered, trying to distract her, "We saw the ferret!"

chapter nine

Charlie made a leap and grabbed the Frisbee out of the air. He loved to play with Frisbees and tennis balls in our backyard.

"Good catch!" I yelled.

"Let me try," Bobby said.

He took the Frisbee from the dog and teased him a bit, then threw it into a long high arch that took it past the open gate and to the side of my house. Charlie bolted through the gate and around the house, out of view. He returned proudly holding the plastic disc in his mouth, like a hunting dog carrying a prized bird.

"See? Charlie catches anything we throw," I said.

Next, I threw a tennis ball. Charlie loved tennis balls. He found more energy from deep down and bolted across the yard to catch the bouncing ball. Mom said he chewed one like a pacifier when he was a little pup, before I was born. Half the time when Charlie napped, he kept a tennis ball in his mouth.

He came back and held his mouth up to me, as if offering for me to take the ball from him. As usual, he pulled away every time I reached for it.

"I think he wants to play keep-away more than he wants to play fetch," I said.

Charlie kept panting, and I wondered what was wrong with him.

"He's really old, for a dog. The summer heat is hard on him. Maybe we should let him rest for a while. I heard every year for a dog is like seven human years. How old is he?" Bobby asked.

"Twelve. And a half," I said.

Bobby took some time and kind of stared off into space, trying to do math in his head.

"That's like a hundred years old! I don't know anyone a hundred years old," he said.

"That can't be right," I said. But it worried me. I walked Charlie to the door, and led him to his water, watching him drink, then settle down to rest.

Outside, I asked Bobby, "Do you think Bandit could fetch things like that?"

"No. Ferrets are like wild animals. Charlie is practically a person. He wouldn't even run off with the gate open," he said, "Bandit's probably gone. I think he's run off to bigger woods far away from here. Either that, or he's living in the storm drain. We would have seen him by now. Maybe we should check in the storm drain??"

"Maybe," I said.

I really wanted to find Bandit, but I didn't want to go into that drain. It scared the crap out of me. The older kids would go in there sometimes, but I would always make excuses to hang back. It was filthy, pitch black, and no one had ever seen where it ended.

Bobby sat down at the picnic table. He pulled some money out of his pocket and spread it out beside him, counting it.

He said, "Come on, Meat."

I followed him around to the front, outside the opened garage. Bobby's bike was at his house, so he hopped on my bike and rode it down the driveway.

I grabbed my sister's bike and chased after him.

Looking back, he said, "Hey, you're good on that one! See if you can catch me!"

I pedaled fast, confident I would maintain control when I stopped.

We kept riding and riding. Before I knew it, I was out of our neighborhood and following through the back roads of Hidden Woods Apartments. I really wanted to turn around, knowing my mom wouldn't want me riding so far from home, but he was on my bike and I was proud that I could keep up with him.

After a long time, we sped across a bigger road then cut through back streets of another community that I wasn't familiar with.

"It's hot, but I have some money. Let's get a coke at the 7-Eleven," he said.

Exhausted and thirsty, I didn't even know where we were, let alone how to reach a 7-Eleven.

"Where is it? I thought the 7-Eleven was the other way," I said.

"Not that one. Just follow me," he said.

So we kept riding. There weren't many hills to climb, but it wore me out. My legs weren't used to pedaling a big bike. My sister sure would be mad if she saw her bike was missing.

Sweating, I yelled for him to stop for a second.

"How much farther? I'm tired," I said.

I didn't want to tell him I was afraid to get caught, or that my sister would beat me up if she knew I had her bike.

"I thought it was closer than this. It can't be too far, now," he said. But he didn't sound confident.

We pedaled for another ten minutes before I finally recognized something. I saw a train track. We followed a trail beside it. It took us to a huge parking lot with an enormous square building. We had driven our bikes all the way to Harundale Mall!

It took a long time to get there, riding with Mom in her car. I never dreamed we had gone so far on our bikes.

"I guess we missed the turn to the 7-Eleven," Bobby said, "but this is cooler! The mall! We can get a soda and check out the pet store."

Nervous to be spotted so far from home, I followed him to the mall entrance. Beside it, there were two other bikes attached to a rack with chains and locks. We put ours beside them, but we didn't have chains.

"We won't be long," he said, "they should be fine."

Sweaty as we were, the air-conditioned mall felt cold as we wandered in. We sat at the little round spinning stools at the counter at the drug store and Bobby bought us both sodas. We drank them fast, thirsty as we were. I kept worrying that someone would recognize me and call my mom.

Walking through the open area of the mall, we passed two long-haired guys and a girl. It seemed like there were always teenagers wandering around inside. When we passed, one of the boys slapped me on the top of my head and stepped in front of me, blocking my way.

"Looks like he's been swimming," he said, poking at my sweaty damp shirt, "They shouldn't let these little kids in here, they stink up the place."

"Leave him alone!" Bobby said, inserting himself between us, even though the teenager was taller than him.

A man behind the pizza counter stopped working and watched.

Aware of his gaze, the boy laughed and walked away, with the other two following him.

"Ya think we should leave?" I asked.

"Don't worry about them, they're just being jerks," Bobby said.

After that we looked in a few shops, but he was determined to go to the Doctor Pet Center and see if he could afford a new pet.

Puppies were playing in the front window.

Parakeets and other birds made squawking noises. The whole place smelled like a hamster cage. There were fish tanks along one wall and other aquariums held guinea pigs, hamsters, and gerbils. The two largest aquariums had huge sleeping snakes. Beside them were about a dozen white mice. There was a sign that read: Mice 88 cents.

"Dude, they give these mice to the snakes to eat!" Bobby said.

"Poor things. Why don't they just feed them dry dog food or something?" I asked.

"I don't think they like it," he said. "Look, I have over two more bucks left... So let's get some mice. We'll save them and let them live like hamsters. I'll let you keep one."

I thought it was a great idea.

The guy at the register gave us our mice in two separate carry-out bowls with lids that had air-holes poked in them. Bobby and I walked out of the mall, looking over our mice, until we reached the bike rack.

Gone. My sister's bike was gone. The two chained bikes were also gone. Frantic, I searched around and, to my relief, my own bike was still on a curb about fifty feet away, laying half in the street. I looked all around the parking lot, but there was no sign of my sister's bike.

"Stolen! Someone swiped her bike!" I yelled, "What am I going to do?"

Bobby used my bike to circle the outside of the entire mall, searching. "It's gone. Those jerks probably took it," he said.

"We gotta tell the store people! Maybe they'll call the police," I said, shaking.

"We can't! I'm not allowed to ride this far, and I KNOW you aren't," Bobby said.

It was a long way home. Bobby let me sit on the back of the bike for most of the way, and we used a bag to tie the mice to the handlebars.

Bobby was quiet for a bit, then said, "When we get home, put your bike away. If anyone asks you, just say we hung out at my house all day. Don't even tell them you borrowed her bike. They'll think it got stolen out of the garage."

I doubted I would get away with it.

No one spotted us when we pulled up to the house and into the garage.

I was afraid my mom would ask where I got the mouse, so Bobby kept it with him, among his zoo of animals.

I had trouble sleeping for a few nights, feeling guilty for keeping this secret, dreading the time that was sure to come when my sister would realize her bike was missing. But days went by and no one even noticed it was gone.

Until one day, I heard her yelling.

"Jimmy! Where's my bike?" she asked.

"I don't know, Last time I saw it, you had it laying outside on the front lawn," I lied.

I pretended to be reading the *Fantastic Four* comic book I had in my lap, when she hauled off and punched me in the side of the head. I jumped up and swung back, missing her. She did a drop-kick, and it thudded into my belly. Tina was three years older than me and took ballet lessons. They should have registered her feet as deadly weapons.

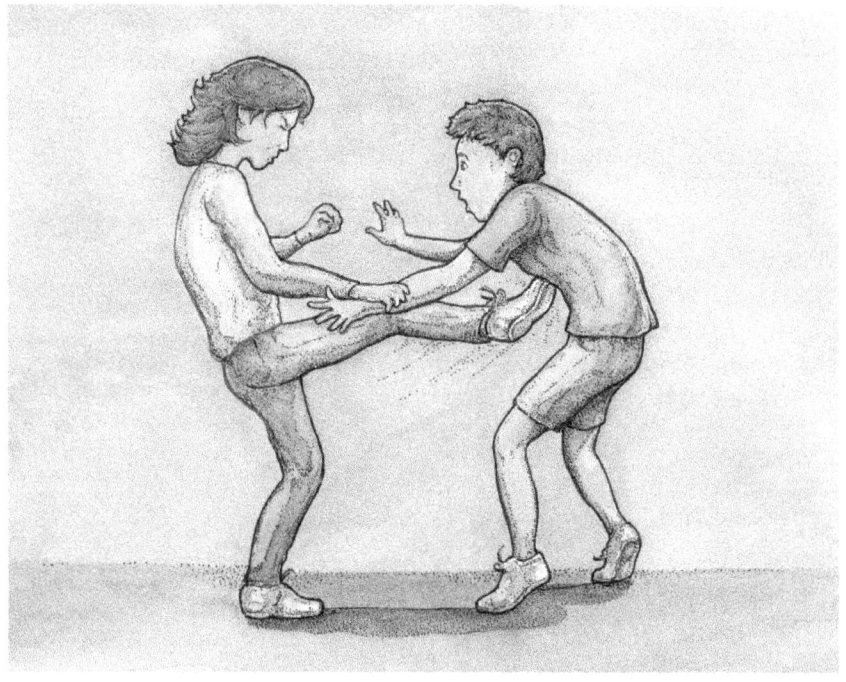

"Where did you leave it?" she screamed.

"Knock it off! I'm telling Mom!" I yelled.

"It was in the garage! You took it!" she said, "Did you leave it at Bobby's house? Where IS IT, Meathead?" she demanded.

I wanted to tell her the truth, I really did, but when she started hitting me and was so mean and hollering, it was easier to lie about it.

It was almost as if she could smell the guilt on me, though. I played dumb. It wasn't long before she realized we would never find it. She accused me of leaving it out in the front yard a thousand times, but I denied it.

Later that night, she was crying about it, and I felt terrible.

"Tina, maybe you're right, maybe I left it out front. I just don't remember doing that," I said.

Mom and Dad assumed someone stole it from the yard or garage. They told me to let her ride mine until they'd replace it on her birthday. Shamefully, I even acted wounded about having to share my bike.

"I know what you did, Meathead, and one day, I will get you back for it," she said.

chapter Ten

"We've never gone far enough to see where it opens up again," Bobby said, "It might go on for miles."

It hadn't rained much lately, so the water running from the mouth of the storm drain was shallow and trickling. Bobby turned his flashlight on, making sure it worked.

We tried to find Bandit for weeks, since he popped out from under that tree, but there was no trace of him.

"I think we should look for him in the storm drain," Bobby said.

The storm drain scared the crap out of me, but I missed my pet, and I hoped we could tame him again. Bobby showed up that morning with a fancy heavy-duty flashlight and assured me we'd be fine.

"What are you scared of? It's just dark. We have a light!" he said.

My shoulder felt wet after it brushed against the side. Bobby's light showed that I had a big black streak on my shirt. One reason I hated the tunnel, the whole interior had a layer of tar on it. Gross.

I felt like the top was going to cave in on my head. The tunnel was four-foot around, but as I went further back, there were globs hanging down from the top, like slimy boogers. I had to bend and duck-walk, or I might get the sticky tar in my hair.

"We shoulda wore hats," I said.

"We will next time," Bobby said.

His flashlight shimmered ahead of us. We were farther back than we'd ever been. The tunnel turned to the left, then continued. Bobby kidded and turned off his light. It was pitch black.

"Quit goofing around!" I demanded.

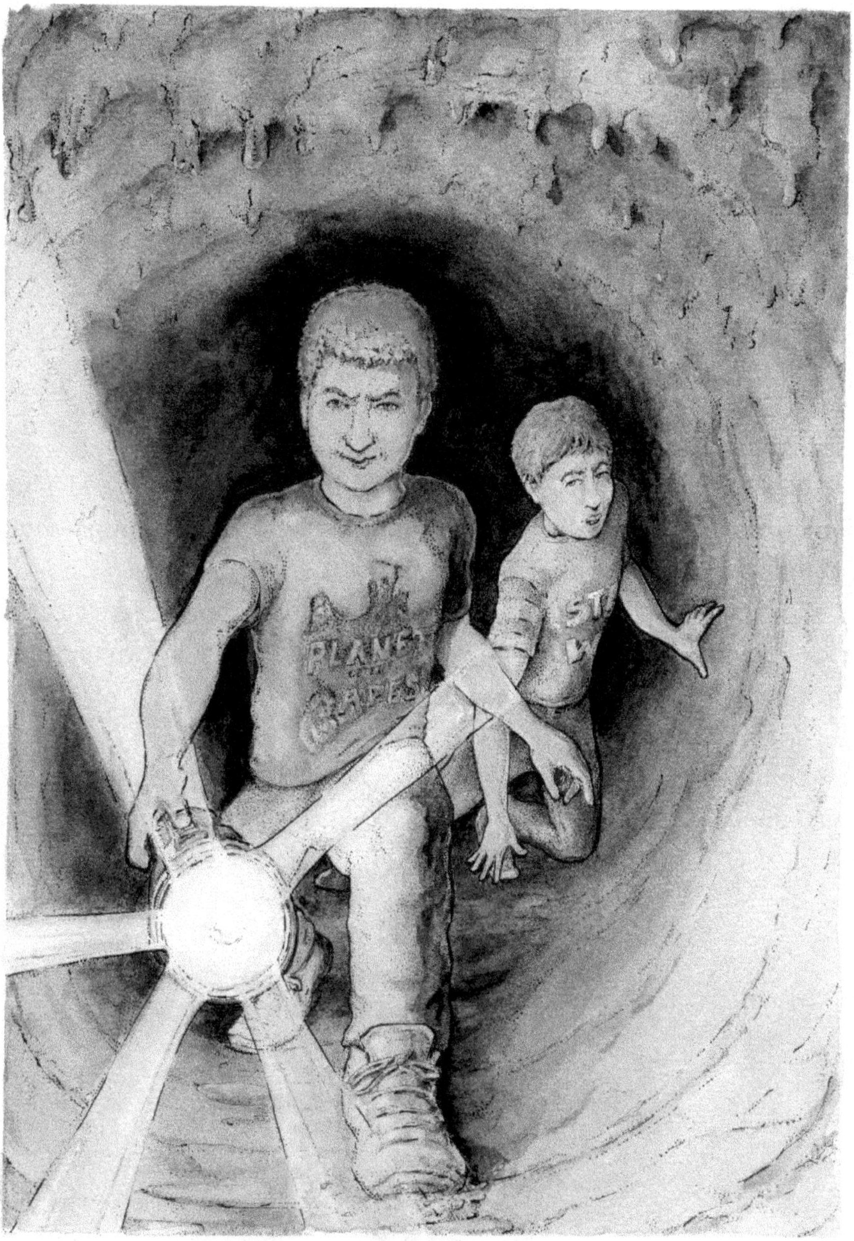
PLANET
APES

I didn't want to seem like a sissy, but it spooked me. He laughed and turned it back on, and we continued our trek through the storm drain.

"We must be on the other side of the highway by now," I said.

That's when we heard a noise. Something scurried around, splashing in the water ahead of us. Bobby aimed the light in my eyes and then back in that direction. Nothing.

His flashlight flickered just as something moved toward it. The light went out again.

"Turn it on!" I yelled, watching him shaking it as the light blinked on and off. The batteries must have been loose inside.

Clump.

Splash!

Whatever it was, it was coming toward us.

"Bandit?" I asked.

Slightly ahead of me, Bobby's light flicked on and off, and I saw something brown and furry moving toward us. I heard another sound behind us, then something brushed against the back of my leg.

Then Bobby's light stayed on. Four or five other sets of eyes gleamed back at us from the darkness. The eyes attached to the brown and furry creature in front belonged to a rat. A big rat!

We both shrieked.

Shining the light beside us, we saw they were behind us, too. Surrounded!

"Ahhh! Go! Go! Go!" Bobby yelled.

He crawled over me like I was a stepping-stool, pushing me down into the muck at the bottom of the tunnel.

Terrified, I jumped up and started duck-walking as fast as I could, convinced something was about to bite me in the dark from behind. Bobby was ahead of me, his flashlight bobbing around, blinking on and off so much that it made me dizzy. We rounded a corner, and I realized how far back we really were. I started into more of a jog with my head and shoulders stooped low.

I bumped my head twice but got out of the storm drain right behind Bobby. The sunlight was so bright compared to that pitch-black tunnel; it made my eyes hurt. I pushed past Bobby and kept running up the hill to my Big Wheel, with Bobby right behind me.

We both stopped and tried to catch our breath.

"They were huge!" Bobby said, out of breath.

Greasy tar and slime from the tunnel covered both of us...

"Rats... can eat... a person alive," Bobby said.

Then we both started laughing.

"You got some tar in your hair!" I said.

He grabbed at the sticky mess. I felt my scalp and pulled my hand back with clinging black streaks on it.

Later, at home in the kitchen, Mom used a pair of scissors to snip big chunks of hair from my head after many failed attempts to remove the tar. In the places she snipped it, I had about a half-inch of hair left. I looked in the mirror and saw I was missing big patches of hair.

"You should just get a crewcut again, a whiffle," Mom said.

"Can't I just wear my baseball cap for a few months?!" I whined.

Mom always wanted me to have short hair. She showed off pictures of my brother and I with those weird whiffle haircuts from years ago. We looked so bald.

"I'll take you later for a haircut, we'll ask the barber what he can do," she said.

Things didn't go my way at the barber shop.

I teared up as the barber turned me around to face the big mirror.

"I look like Gomer Pyle," I complained, "It's awful!"

"You look fine, son. Like a gentleman," he said.

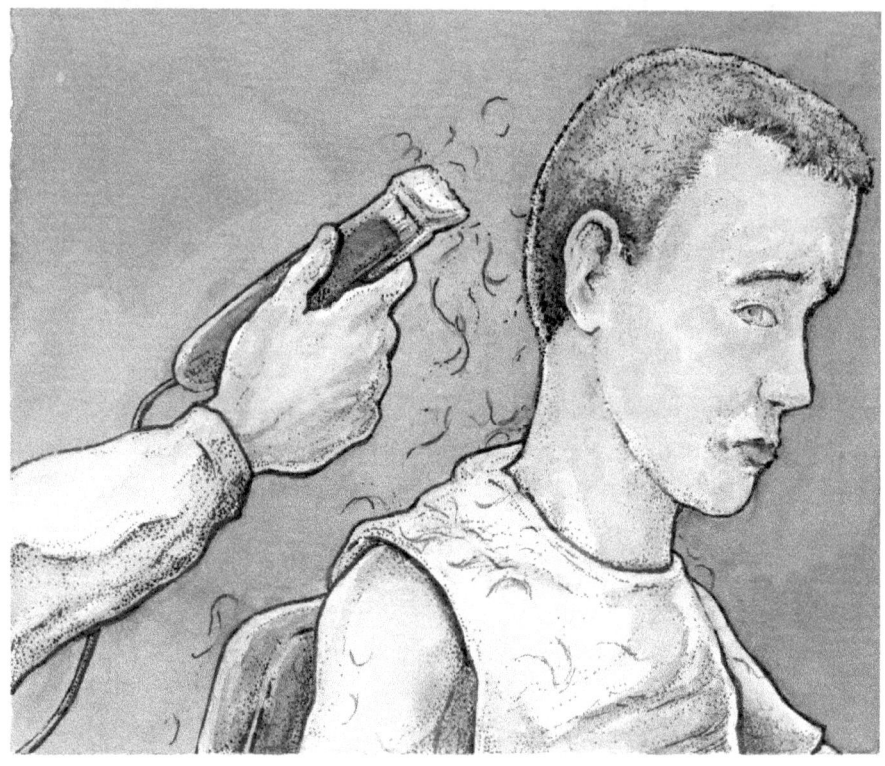

He'd used vibrating clippers to shave my head down to about a quarter inch of hair. I hated whiffles.

And I did wear my Orioles cap, practically all the time. It would be months before school started back up, and I had longer hair, about an inch high, which was still too short of a haircut, but at least it wasn't a whiffle.

Chapter Eleven

It was a Saturday morning, and I sat watching TV with Mom and Dad.

"I'm worried about Charlie," Mom said, "He's not himself. He barely wants to play and sleeps all the time."

Dad said, "Maybe he ate something bad for him outside."

"I'm going to take him to the vet's if he doesn't start getting better soon," she said.

Doctor Hartman, the veterinarian, was an animal doctor who always helped Charlie when he was sick.

"You don't feel good, boy?" she asked him.

Charlie was loving and protective of our entire family, but he really loved Mom. Wherever Mom went, he followed, like they were connected at the hip. He'd lay on her bed and whine when she left the house.

She pet his head. He wagged his tail a little and curled up on her lap, gripping a tennis ball in his mouth.

He seemed almost back to normal the next day. Still, he wasn't eating as much as he used to. Mom watched him closely for the next few days.

At the end of the week, it surprised me when Charlie didn't come to the door when I got home from school. He always did. But not that day. At dinner the night before, he wouldn't eat his food at all.

Mom and Dad took him to the veterinarian while we were at school, and they said he had something called tumors. It was hurting him so much that they had to let him go to sleep. Mom said he wouldn't be hurting anymore.

Dad was home from work and my brother and sister were already out of school, sobbing in the living room.

Mom cried; I think it was the first time I ever saw her cry. We sat around the living room and told stories about him and how much we loved him. It didn't seem like he was a pet; more like he was a person. I couldn't believe he was gone.

All my friends and neighbors said they were sorry that he died, and Miss Sandy next door told me she was sorry I lost a member of my family.

"There will never be another Charlie," Mom said.

Mom laid around on her bed like Charlie used to do when he worried that she wouldn't come back home.

We put Charlie's tennis ball on the fireplace mantle next to a box with his ashes in it. Every time I ever saw a tennis ball, I thought of our dog, Charlie.

chapter twelve

I thought about Charlie for a long time, missing him.

It was a Saturday night, and I hung out with Bobby at his house. We played with the snake, mice, and frogs.

Bobby said, "It sucks that pets have to die, but that's how God made them. They just don't live as long as people."

"He was the best dog ever," I answered.

I took care to handle Bobby's pets gently. After losing Charlie, I realized more and more that these animals weren't prizes, that they were fragile and unique.

We were making a home for his new iguana in the garage. We placed a piece of bark and long branches into an aquarium full of grass, with paper towels lining the bottom. The vented top had a big heat lamp that ran the length of it.

I agreed to stay over at Bobby's. It used to terrify me that I'd pee the bed if I slept over at anyone's house. But I'd been doing a lot better with it lately. It had been weeks since my last accident, so when he asked if I would spend the night, I decided it would be safe. I was wrong.

We stayed up late, finishing the cage.

"This is nice, Jimmy. You never spend the night over here," Bobby's mom said, turning out the light.

I woke up in the middle of the night and to my horror, I had wet the bed. Bobby slept in another bed across the room. I laid there for over an hour, tearing up at the idea that all my friends would know how gross I was.

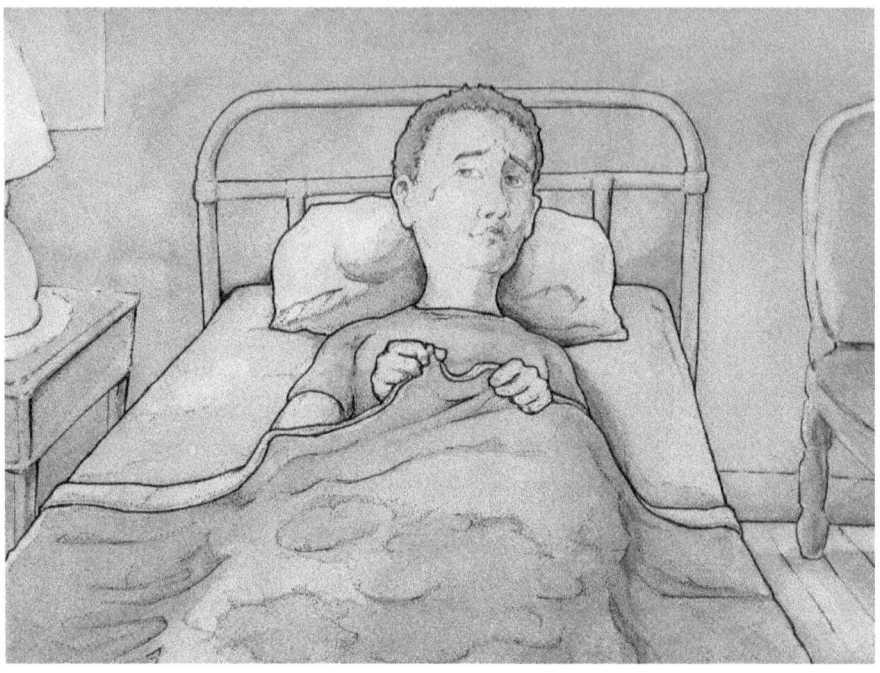

"You awake?" Bobby asked.

He probably heard me whimpering. "Yeah... I... um... I had an accident." I decided there was no way around it, so I would come clean. "Your Mom is going to hate me. I peed the bed." I confessed.

Bobby laughed a little and called his mom to the room. She was very sweet about it and let me sleep on the couch for the rest of the night, after giving me a pair of Bobby's shorts to wear.

Cursed, just like the gypsy lady said.

I didn't sleep much. I worried Bobby would tell all the guys and goof on me relentlessly. I imagined they would make up an even weirder nickname for me. I could almost hear them calling me Peeboy or Wizzkid for the rest of my life.

Awkward and humiliated, I snuck out early and went home.

Later that day, the guys were riding around my court on their bikes. I avoided them, staying inside.

When they were gone, I pulled my bike out of the garage and got on. All the practice was starting to pay off. I fell once when I came to a stop, but then I learned to control my speed and balance enough to settle to the pavement gently.

I rode alone, thinking about Charlie. I even got up the nerve to take the trail at the other end of the community to the faraway pond. I set the bike down in the weeds and walked the rest of the way to check out the pond.

Alone, I crept up and spotted a huge frog. I dashed my hand out and caught him. He wasn't as big as the one Bobby saw last time, but he was the biggest frog I ever caught. I held him for a bit, and considered riding home with him. But, I didn't want to hurt him, so I let him go. I placed him at the water's edge and watched him hop off into the depths.

Riding back home, I felt a strange pride for having gone such a long way alone. I bet I could find my way to Harundale Mall by myself if I tried.

I still dreaded hearing my friends bust on me about peeing the bed. But, for some reason, it didn't seem so important, anymore. I knew I would be okay.

After school the next day, when Matt, Bobby, and Michael came to the door with their bikes, I joined them.

I kept waiting for Bobby to bring up peeing the bed, but he didn't. We rode around the block a few times and all the way up Phirne Road. I told them about the frog I caught and let go, but I don't think they believed me. I think I impressed them with my bike riding abilities, though.

After Matt and Michael left for dinner, I finally brought it up.

"Did you ever tell those guys about me peeing the bed?" I asked.

"No. No, Jimmy, I didn't," he said, "I used to do it, too. I still do, sometimes. But don't tell anybody, okay?"

"Okay," I said.

If Bobby peed the bed too, what was the big deal? I couldn't believe it. All this time I was so scared of my friends finding out, but instead of being ashamed, I kind of felt proud that someone I looked up to so much had the same problem.

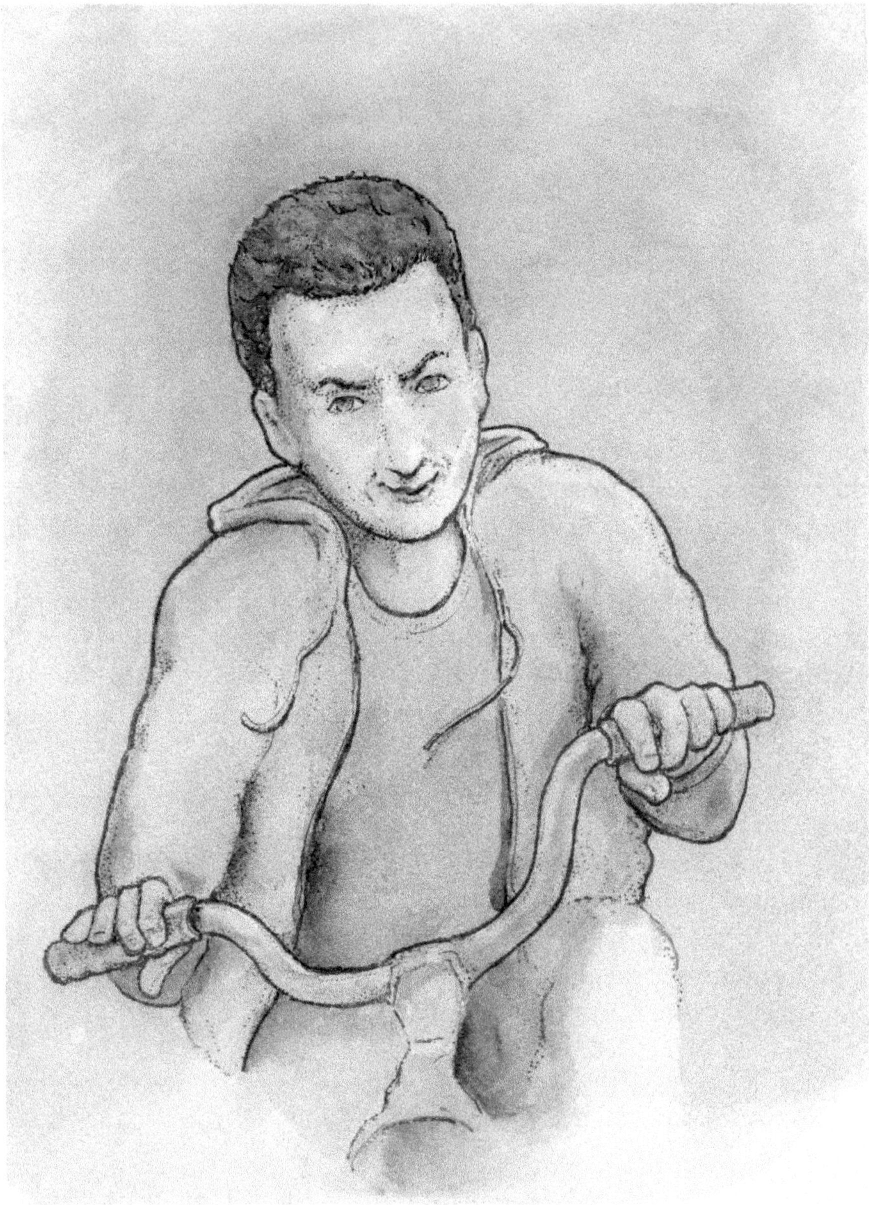

Chapter Thirteen

I was happy to help Mom pull the plastic covers off my bed. It had been a long time since my accident at Bobby's house. Mom decided I wasn't such a huge danger to saturate the mattress in my sleep. Keeping the windows closed to the noisy planes seemed to help, and I always used the bathroom right before going to bed. She also made me go to bed earlier every night, to get more sleep. It seemed to work.

I realized there probably wasn't a curse on me. Maybe I just watched too many scary movies.

She pulled the whole bedframe out from the side wall and corner, and I picked up a nugget of Charlie's old dry dog food from under the edge of the carpet.

"Bandit must have hidden that there last year," Mom said, "He hoarded it everywhere! I still find pieces around the house."

It had been a very long time, an entire year since my pet ferret left the house.

I felt closer to Mom. No longer wetting the bed, it was like we won a contest or defeated an enemy together.

"Mom, I have something to tell you. I kind of think I borrowed Tina's other bike and left it outside when it got stolen," I confessed.

"Oh, really? And why didn't you tell us that, Jimmy? I should punish you! She's very careful with her bike," Mom said, "... but don't tell her that, now. She'll kill you."

And I didn't.

Later, my sister Tina came in from the garage. She had a tiny key in her hand. For her birthday, Mom and Dad bought her a fancy new ten-speed bike. It was a little too tall for her, and way too big for me, even though I'd gotten better at riding my bike without crashing. She had a chain with a small padlock for the bike, keeping it safe from thieves. Safe from me.

"You keep your hands off my new bike," she said.

"Of course I will. Still, I really do need to learn how to ride a ten-speed," I said, tormenting her, "All the bigger kids are getting ten-speeds."

Honestly, big ten-speeds terrified me, but I wouldn't let her know that.

"Just stay away from it, Meathead!" she said.

Later, sitting on the couch watching *Spider-Man* cartoons, I heard a noise at the back door.

Through the glass, it startled me to see Bandit sniffing at the door. He was bigger, with lots of white hair.

"Food! You want some food, boy?" I asked.

Upstairs, I filled a bowl from the bag of Charlie's old dog food. I brought it out. He was still waiting there.

First, I offered a piece from my hand. He didn't take it, but he didn't run, either.

Like Bobby said, Bandit was a wild animal now. I was going to have to accept it and let him go, but I would always look for him to return to our back door for a meal.

I laid the bowl on the patio in front of the door a few feet from him and he carefully approached, taking one nugget at a time. He paused a second and looked me in the eye. I wondered, is he just hungry, or does he remember me?

I stepped out and walked along with him through the grass. He lingered with me a bit, then slowly made his way across the yard, off to the woods, and down the gully.

afterword

I drove to the old neighborhood recently. Parking my truck, I walked down the hill beside my old house to the gully. Looking around, everything seemed smaller than I recalled.

Still, the smell of skunk cabbage and honeysuckles filled the air, just like the old days. A squirrel bounced around the top of an oak tree, and robins fluttered, pecking at the grass along the hillside. But there were no signs of any frogs in the water trickling at the bottom. This couldn't possibly be the stream from my memories. This little drainage ditch seemed to be a different place altogether. Then I looked into the tunnels and remembered.

Slipping out of the cherry tree and chipping my teeth in a rough landing. Spraining my ankle after leaping from the top of the tunnels on a dare. A fist fight with an older friend, after finally digging up the courage to stand up for myself. Finding a stray cat and feeding him, eventually to take him home. A thousand times, catching frogs and toads. And the forts. Underground, in the trees, alongside the stream.

Those memories, and the stories in this book, made one thing clear. The gully is still an enormous place for me. It contains trials and errors; successes and failures; it holds adventures and dreams, all in the little details of my childhood memories.

acknowledgments

I've always been encouraged to be creative by my friends. But some have stood out and become mentors to me in my artwork and writing.

I would like to thank Billy Snyder, Jeff Antkowiak, Lew Hartman, Jonathon Fuqua, Gerald Hausman, and Jane Lindskold for all their help, guidance, and suggestions over the years. It means a lot to me.

Special thanks to Roxy, Sammy, and Jimmy. Jimmy, you are the best editor my money can buy.

Finally, thanks to Reagan Rothe at Black Rose Writing for believing in this book.

about the author

James B. Zimmerman lives with his wife Roxanna in the mountains of western Maryland. He has written and illustrated two Meathead books, *Growing up Meathead* (2020 NYC Big Book Award Distinguished Favorite,) and his new book, *Down the Gully.* He has illustrated the classic written works of Roger Zelazny, Jules Verne, Robert E. Howard, and many others in books and magazines. For more information, go to *JimZimmermanart.com.*

note from the author

Word-of-mouth is crucial for any author to succeed. If you enjoyed *Down the Gully*, please leave a review online—anywhere you are able. Even if it's just a sentence or two. It would make all the difference and would be very much appreciated.

Thanks!
James B. Zimmerman

Thank you so much for reading one of
James B Zimmerman's novels.
If you enjoyed the experience, please check out our recommended
title for your next great read!

Growing up Meathead

"A sweet snapshot of a 1970s suburban American childhood."
–IndieReader

View other Black Rose Writing titles at
www.blackrosewriting.com/books and use promo code
PRINT to receive a **20% discount** when purchasing.

CPSIA information can be obtained
at www.ICGtesting.com
Printed in the USA
BVHW062153121021
618743BV00011B/449

9 781684 337873